DATE DUE			

Trustworthiness

By Bruce S. Glassman

With an Introduction by
Michael Josephson,
Founder of CHARACTER COUNTS!SM

JOSEPHSON
INSTITUTE
CHARACTERCOUNTS!

Produced and created in partnership with Josephson Institute

Special Thanks goes to the following people, whose help on this project was invaluable:

At CHARACTER COUNTS!:
Michael Josephson
Rich Jarc
Amanda Skinner
Mimi Drop
Michelle Del Castillo

Content Advisers:
Dave Bender, book publisher
Tracy Hughes, educator
& CHARACTER COUNTS!
coordinator for Meadowbrook
Middle School, San Diego
Cindy De Clercq, Elementary
School Principal

And thanks to:
Nathan Glassman-Hughes,
Emma Glassman-Hughes,
Natalia Mata, Erica Warren,
Ebony Sanders, Kellen
O'Connell, Nicole Rigler,
and Alex Olberding

Library of Congress Cataloging-in-Publication Data

Glassman, Bruce.
Trustworthiness / written by Bruce S. Glassman. — 1st ed.
p. cm. — (Six Pillars of Character series)
Includes bibliographical references and index.
ISBN-13: 978-1-60108-510-8 (hardcover); ISBN-10: 1-60108-510-9 (hardcover)
ISBN-13: 978-1-60108-511-5 (pbk.); ISBN-10: 1-60108-511-7 (pbk.)
1. Reliability—Juvenile literature. I. Title.

BJ1500.T78G53 2009
179'.9—dc22   2008001193
Printed in China

Contents

Introduction: Michael Josephson 4

Chapter 1: What Is Trustworthiness? 10

Chapter 2: The Importance of Trustworthiness 30

Chapter 3: Trustworthiness in Your Life 38

Glossary 47

Resources 47

Index 48

Photo Credits 48

Ethics play a part in more daily decisions than you may think. The test-taking scenario is only one example of an ethical choice.

You are faced with ethical choices every day. One of the main goals of this series is to show you how to recognize which choices are ethical choices. Another main goal is to show you how to make the right ethical choices.

About Being Ethical

Being ethical isn't simply about what is allowed—or legal—and what is not. You can often find a legal way to do what is unethical. Maybe you saw that a cashier at the grocery store forgot to ring up one of your items. There is no law that says you must tell him or her. But, is it ethical to just walk out without mentioning it? The answer is no. You're still being dishonest by taking something you did not pay for.

So, being ethical is about something more than "what you can get away with." It is about what you do because *you know it's the right thing to do*—regardless of who's watching and regardless of whether you may stand to gain. Often there is a price to pay for doing the right thing.

Character Takes Courage

There are many obstacles to being ethical—chances are you're faced with some of them every day. Maybe you don't want to be

There are many obstacles to being ethical. Overcoming them takes courage and hard work.

embarrassed by telling the truth. Or maybe you feel doing the right thing will take too much effort. Few good things come without a cost. Becoming a person of character is hard work. Here is a poem I wrote that makes this point.

chapter 1

What Is Trustworthiness?

A great deal of our world is built on trust.

Think about the world at large. How do all the world's people get along? For one thing, nations only exist peacefully together if they have a mutual trust in each other. Each must feel secure that their neighbors and others in the world community do not threaten them. Leaders and governments only feel secure when they see that other nations keep their promises and do what they say they will do.

Your community—your city, town, or neighborhood—also runs on trust. The very laws by which we live require us to uphold shared

Trust forms the foundation of most human interactions.

Public Trust Betrayed

One of the most important trusts we have as citizens is the trust we place in our government. When we elect public officials, we entrust them with great power. We trust them to work in our best interest. When that trust is betrayed, it threatens the very core of our society. Consider the story of Randy "Duke" Cunningham:

Randy "Duke" Cunningham was a California congressman. He represented the citizens of Southern California for more than 15 years. In 2005, Cunningham resigned his office after pleading guilty to bribery. He admitted that, while he was in office, he "sold" his influence. That means—in return for money, gifts, and other valuable things—Cunningham agreed to help certain businesess and business leaders. He agreed to support and vote for things that helped the people who paid him. All in all, Cunningham took more than $2 million in bribes.

"The truth is I broke the law," Cunningham said in his resignation speech. "I concealed my conduct and disgraced my office. I know I will forfeit my reputation, my worldly possessions—most importantly the trust of my friends and family."

Cunningham's story is a sad one. But it shows how one betrayal can affect so many people on so many levels. With his dishonesty, Cunningham let down his family, his friends, his fellow congressmen, and the people who

Congressman Randy "Duke" Cunningham resigned in disgrace after he was caught taking millions of dollars in bribes.

elected him. As U.S. Attorney Carol Lam said, "The citizens who elected Cunningham assumed that he would do his best for them. Instead, he did the worst thing an elected official can do—he enriched himself through his position and violated the trust of those that put him there."

Sincerity. The key to sincerity is being genuine. That means speaking without an intention to mislead or leave the wrong impression—even if you don't actually say anything that's not true. Many people use insincerity for what they believe is a "good cause." They use insincerity as a way to avoid hurting someone else's feelings. Here's a good story about insincerity:

A grateful parent showed up at soccer practice one day with pie she had baked for the coach. The coach thanked her for her kindness and promised to take the pie home that night and have it for dessert with his family. That night, after dinner, the pie was served. The look on everyone's face after taking the first bite was unmistakable. The pie was absolutely awful.

As the coach's family politely spit the pie into their dinner napkins, the coach got up and threw the pie in the trash.

After the next practice, the grateful parent came up to the coach and eagerly asked him, "So, coach. What did you think of my pie?"

The coach made it a habit not to lie, so he replied, "Well, I tell you, pies like that don't last very long in our house!"

Feeling good, the grateful parent thanked the coach again and went on her way.

His intentions were good, but was the coach dishonest? Did he mislead the parent with his answer, even though his words were literally true?

There are many times when we are tempted to use words that are intentionally "fuzzy" in order to avoid conflict or unease. But, are we really doing a service to the other person or people? Most of the time the answer is no. If we have intentionally given a wrong impression, we have been dishonest.

Candor. Silence can be a form of dishonesty. In your important relationships, you likely have an expectation—a trust—that others will tell you something if it's important. This is also called an expectation of forthrightness or frankness. As an honest person, you have an obligation to volunteer information that you know is important to another person. Here's a good story about not being candid:

> Rick just found out that Emma is going to the Halloween Dance with a boy named Eric.
>
> Rick's best friend, Donny, has told Rick a hundred times that he has a huge crush on Emma. For months, Donny has been trying to get the courage to ask Emma to the dance.
>
> Later in the day, Donny runs up to Rick with a huge smile on his face. He's decided that today he will ask Emma to the dance. Rick considers telling Donny what he knows, but he doesn't want to disappoint his friend. So he remains silent. Donny then runs off to ask Emma the big question.

Was Rick's silence honest?

It was "well meaning," but the answer is no. As friends, Rick and Donny have expectations of each other. One expectation is that each will be candid with the other. That means, if you have information or feedback that you know would be important to the other person, you have a duty to tell them. Not doing so is dishonest.

Honesty in Conduct

Honesty in conduct is about being honest in your actions. It means playing by the rules. It also means no stealing, cheating, or trickery. It means—for example—when your tennis opponent hits that final shot deep just barely on the baseline—you'll call it "good." Even if you are the only one who saw it. And even if it means losing the match.

Honest conduct means consistently doing the right thing—even when no one else is watching.

Anne Frank, Miep Gies, and an Ethical Lie

During World War II (1939 to 1945), countries across the globe fought the threat of Adolf Hitler and his Nazi party. Hitler and his Nazi forces invaded or took over many countries in Europe, including Austria, Poland, Hungary, Czechoslovakia, Russia, France, and the Netherlands. One of the Nazis' stated goals was to rid the world of Jews.

In Amsterdam, in 1942, a family of Jews went into hiding to escape capture by the Nazis. Businessman Otto Frank moved his wife and two daughters—Margot and Anne—into a hidden room above his office. For 25 months, the Franks stayed only within the walls of their hideaway.

One of the people who helped the Franks survive was a woman named Miep Gies. She made sure they had food and water. And, when questioned by the Nazis, she lied in order to protect the lives that were entrusted to her.

In helping the hidden Jews, Miep was not only being kind, she was also risking her own safety. People who hid or helped Jews were threatened by the Nazis with severe punishment— even death. But Miep did not feel she had a choice. She said:

> *My decision to help Otto was because I saw no alternative. I could foresee many sleepless nights and an unhappy life if I*

refused. And that was not the kind of failure I wanted for myself. Permanent remorse about failing to do your human duty, in my opinion, can be worse than losing your life.

Miep Gies risked her own life by lying to protect Jews during World War II.

There were many times when turning the Franks in would have been in Miep's best self-interest. But her beliefs never waivered. "I never considered betraying the Franks," she once said in an interview, "whatever benefit this might have meant for me."

Anne Frank and her family were eventually found and captured. They were sent to prison camps, where Anne, her mother, and sister eventually died. Only Otto Frank survived the war.

After the war, Anne Frank's now famous diary was published. Miep's courage and character became known around the world. Miep was honored for her bravery and humanitarianism by many organizations. She was even knighted by the queen of the Netherlands. Despite all the honors, Miep Gies insisted she did nothing exceptional. "I am not a hero," she often said, "I just did what any decent person would have done."

Loyalty is a trait we all value.

this in the future? Am I sure the other person is clear about exactly what I'm promising? Keeping promises realistic and clear helps to keep everyone's communication honest.

Loyalty

Chances are you are part of many different kinds of relationships. Some are with your close family and best friends. These give you access to private information about others. As a loyal person, you have an obligation to keep that information confidential. So, just as candor requires that you provide information in certain situations, loyalty demands that you don't share certain information with certain people.

Of course, there are limitations to loyalty. Your loyalty cannot come before your ethics, your personal safety, or the safety of others. Sometimes, you must share sensitive information and disregard a promise of loyalty for a higher purpose. In some cases, someone may have asked for your loyalty but, in doing so, they are asking you to

A loyal person has an obligation to keep private information confidential.

be dishonest or to hide the truth. It is also possible that someone you love will ask you to keep a secret about a crime, a lie, or physical abuse. These are also cases in which your loyalty is less important than getting the truth out in the open.

chapter **2**

The Importance of Trustworthiness

The first line of Chapter 1 bears repeating again here: A great deal of our world is built on trust.

To create a safe society, people and institutions must be trustworthy. Elected officials and government leaders must act ethically. Police officers and other members of law enforcement must be guided by honesty and integrity. The principals and teachers at our schools must also be honest, reliable, and show integrity. When these people are not trustworthy—when they lie, cheat, or disregard promises—their community unravels.

The United Nations strives to build trust and cooperation among all nations of the world.

Gandhi showed great integrity—he was loyal, kept promises, and was always truthful.

march peacefully. He led nation-wide boycotts (organized refusals to purchase certain goods or to use certain services). He also used the weapon of self-sacrifice to call attention to his causes. He would, for instance, go on a hunger strike for weeks in order to make his demands heard. A few times, he starved himself to the brink of death.

Mahatma Gandhi stayed true to his belief in nonviolence no matter what the consequences were. He was imprisoned many times—often in terrible and harsh conditions. He was beaten, and, at one point, attacked by a mob that was going to lynch him. He witnessed the murders and beatings of countless fellow Indians, but he never waivered in his actions.

As a pillar of trustworthiness, Mohandas Gandhi exhibited all the important traits of honesty, loyalty, promise-keeping, and—above all—integrity. His allegiance to honesty and candor was legendary among all who knew him.

One of Gandhi's core values was that of *satyagraha*, which is "devotion to truth." He was honest with anyone who asked him about the potential consequences of nonviolent protest. Often, his answers were not what people wanted to hear. But Gandhi only dealt in the truth. Gandhi himself said, "Truth is what the voice within tells you."

For decades, Gandhi remained fiercely loyal to his causes, especially to nonviolence. He had made a promise never to employ violence in his struggles, and he never did.

Gandhi remained dedicated to nonviolent protest for his entire life.

"My Life Is My Message"

The solid and unchanging relationship between Gandhi's ethics and his actions was perhaps his greatest strength of all. It is what made him such a shining example of integrity. Many people disagreed with Gandhi and his methods. No one, however, ever denied that the man

The same can be said for friendships. Without trust on both sides, a long-term friendship cannot last.

Think about the four key principles of trustworthiness:

1. Honesty   3. Promise-keeping
2. Integrity   4. Loyalty

Are there any of these principles you wouldn't want your parent or best friend to have?

Trust Can Be Fragile

Trust is built over time. In your relationships, it will grow stronger with every action that shows your commitment to it. As others prove they are worthy of trust—one action at a time—you will grow to trust them more as well.

Trust can be fragile. While it can take a long time to build, it can take a very short time to dissolve. Sometimes, all it takes is one deceit to ruin an otherwise trusting relationship.

Consider this story about honesty and trust:

> *Marcia Bennett had recently turned 13. She had been talking to her mom for a while about having more independence. Marcia wanted to be allowed to*

do more things on her own, with just her friends.

One Friday after school, Marcia told her mom that a bunch of friends were going to the movies together at the mall. Could Marcia go with them?

Mrs. Bennett decided this would be a good opportunity for Marcia to be a little more independent. She said yes, but she wanted to know which movie they would see. "We're not sure yet," Marcia said.

"Well, I know that you and I have seen PG-13 movies together," Mrs. Bennett explained, "but when you're out with just your friends, it has to be a PG movie. Got it?" Marcia eagerly agreed.